LEAD AT ANY LEVEL®

SURVIVING THE
LABOR
CRISIS

by Amy C. Waninger

317-589-5955
info@LeadAtAnyLevel.com

Printed in the United States of America
First Printing, 2023

ISBN: 978-1-953640-20-8 (paperback)
ISBN: 978-1-953640-21-5 (Kindle edition)

A Page Beyond
11650 Olio Road, Suite 1000 #392
Fishers, IN 46037
www.APageBeyond.com

a page beyond ™

Ordering Information:
Special discounts are available on quantity purchases by corporations, associations, and others who purchase directly from the copyright holder. Contact info@leadatanylevel.com for details.

Contents

Introduction

Despite the popular claims that "no one wants to work anymore," there really is a worker shortage in the United States. You're not imagining it; it is hard to find good help these days. This makes the cost of turnover even higher for companies—and the return on investment in retention strategies even more compelling.

Understanding where the workers have gone and why they are leaving is at the heart of weathering this crisis. It's not as simple as a better vetting process or a more aggressive bonus structure. Executives need to adapt not only to a smaller pool of applicants, but to a changing zeitgeist in how their employees view employment. Key factors that can address and meet these challenges are retention, inclusion, and engagement.

But first, let's talk about where the workers went and why they're not sticking around.

What's Causing the Worker Shortage: Where Did 5 Million Workers Go?

U.S. news outlets began reporting about a significant worker shortage in Q1 2022. A March 29 CNBC report showed that the U.S. had 5 million more open positions than available workers.[1] We've heard lots of people (many of them either hiring managers or retirees) complain that people are lazy and "don't want to work." But there's more to the story than 5 million people suddenly realizing they would rather binge-watch Netflix than go to work every day.

We've uncovered four factors that more than account for the 5 million missing workers. None of them should surprise us. But we need to change the damaging "lazy worker" narrative to have any hope of addressing the real problems.

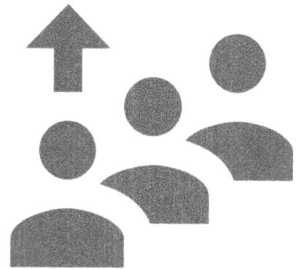

1 JeffCoxCNBCcom. (2022, March 29). There are now a record 5 million more job openings than unemployed people in the U.S. CNBC. Retrieved November 11, 2022, from https://www.cnbc.com/2022/03/29/there-are-now-a-record-5-million-more-job-openings-than-unemployed-people-in-the-us.html

1. Baby Boomers Are Retiring

Remember the "retirement wave" conversations we were having before 2020?[2] Every day ushered in ten thousand new Baby Boomers who were "just one bad day away from retirement."[3]

Still, some people wondered if the Baby Boomers would ever really retire. It turns out, experts were right on track with their predictions. Retirement numbers increased steadily for almost a decade,[4] with the rate of increase slowing a bit in 2019. But then in 2020, the number of new retirees increased by a whopping 3.2 million over the prior year, and still showed a marked increase relative to the overall trend. These "extra" retirees alone comprise 64 percent of the 5 million missing workers.

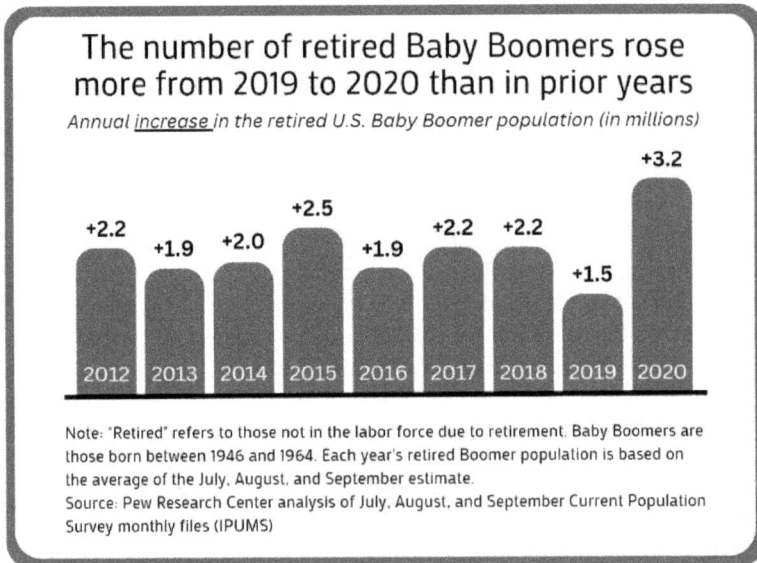

The number of retired Baby Boomers rose more from 2019 to 2020 than in prior years

Annual *increase* in the retired U.S. Baby Boomer population (in millions)

Year	Increase
2012	+2.2
2013	+1.9
2014	+2.0
2015	+2.5
2016	+1.9
2017	+2.2
2018	+2.2
2019	+1.5
2020	+3.2

Note: "Retired" refers to those not in the labor force due to retirement. Baby Boomers are those born between 1946 and 1964. Each year's retired Boomer population is based on the average of the July, August, and September estimate.
Source: Pew Research Center analysis of July, August, and September Current Population Survey monthly files (IPUMS)

2 Boomers' retirement wave likely to begin in just 6 years. PRB. (n.d.). Retrieved November 11, 2022, from https://www.prb.org/resources/boomers-retirement-wave-likely-to-begin-in-just-6-years/
3 Haass, D. (2020, November 24). Council post: Retirement trends of baby boomers. Forbes. Retrieved November 11, 2022, from https://www.forbes.com/sites/forbesfinancecouncil/2019/09/03/retirement-trends-of-baby-boomers/?sh=7ae9ae757378
4 Fry, R. (2020, November 10). The pace of Boomer retirements has accelerated in the past year. Pew Research Center. Retrieved November 11, 2022, from https://www.pewresearch.org/fact-tank/2020/11/09/the-pace-of-boomer-retirements-has-accelerated-in-the-past-year/

2. Immigration Has Plummeted

Whether immigration policy really changes from one presidential administration to the next is up for debate.[5] But the impacts of the pandemic on immigration are undeniable. Non-tourist visas dropped by roughly 50 percent in 2020. And we saw about 50 percent fewer new-arrival green card holders that year.

Together, that's up to 1.2 million foreign workers who didn't come to the U.S. in 2020 alone.

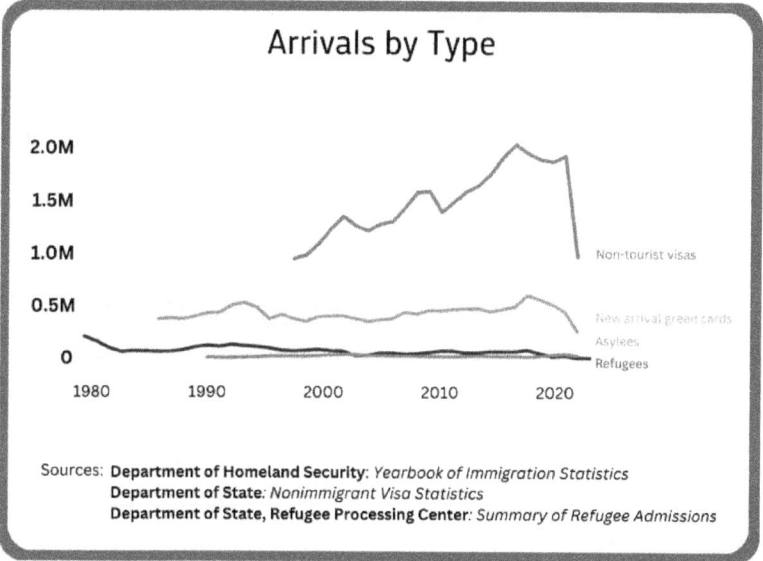

Arrivals by Type

2.0M	
1.5M	
1.0M	Non-tourist visas
0.5M	New arrival green cards
0	Asylees
	Refugees

1980   1990   2000   2010   2020

Sources: **Department of Homeland Security**: *Yearbook of Immigration Statistics*
Department of State: *Nonimmigrant Visa Statistics*
Department of State, Refugee Processing Center: *Summary of Refugee Admissions*

5 Muzaffar Chishti, J. B. M. C. and J. B. (2021, June 8). The "Trump Effect" on legal immigration levels: More perception than reality? migrationpolicy.org. Retrieved November 11, 2022, from https://www.migrationpolicy.org/article/trump-effect-immigration-reality

3. Service Sector Wages Are Rising

As recently as 2021, Reuters reported that the percentage of U.S. workers who held multiple jobs was still rising[6] But something interesting started happening later that year that may have caused a change. Wages, specifically in the service sector, increased significantly. Would this cause a worker shortage? Not exactly, but let me explain why I think it's showing up that way.

Rising Wages May Be Long Overdue

The federal minimum wage has held steady at $7.75 per hour since 2009[7] Some economists suggest that a floor of $20 or more would be necessary to keep pace with inflation[8] State and local governments have countered this stagnation (and boosted their payroll tax revenues) by setting their own minimum wage guidelines[9]

But with workers in high demand, especially in low-wage, service-industry jobs, companies have raised starting wages. Late in 2021, we started seeing signs for $12 per hour starting pay at our local McDonald's. (They've since increased to $15 an hour, adding childcare and weekly pay incentives.) Of course, wage fluctuations vary by industry, and gains to workers may yet be offset by rising inflation.[10, 11]

> *"But with workers in high demand, especially in low-wage, service industry jobs, companies have raised starting wages."*

6 Marte, J., & Mutikani, L. (2021, February 17). Share of U.S. workers holding multiple jobs is rising, new census report shows. Reuters. Retrieved November 11, 2022, from https://www.reuters.com/article/us-usa-economy-multiple-jobs/share-of-u-s-workers-holding-multiple-jobs-is-rising-new-census-report-shows-idUSKBN2AH2PI

7 Minimum wage. United States Department of Labor. (n.d.). Retrieved November 11, 2022, from https://www.dol.gov/agencies/whd/minimum-wage

8 Constant, P. (n.d.). American workers would make more than $20 an hour if minimum wage kept pace with productivity, an economist says. Business Insider. Retrieved November 11, 2022, from https://www.businessinsider.com/minimum-wage-27-if-kept-pace-productivity-economist-opinion-2022-4

9 The Economist Newspaper. (n.d.). The federal minimum wage is becoming irrelevant. The Economist. Retrieved November 11, 2022, from https://www.economist.com/united-states/2019/04/27/the-federal-minimum-wage-is-becoming-irrelevant?utm_medium=cpc.adword.pd&utm_source=google&utm_campaign=a.22brand_pmax&utm_content=conversion.direct-response.anonymous&gclid=CjwKCAjwy_aUBhACEiwA2IHHQMpZRNOCu62PMzV7g4fHUdlvwDWYpy2bEJ2l8kTbdBrlB5r4Ei28rRoCrpwQAvD_BwE

10 Popli, N. (2022, February 3). These industries saw the greatest pay increases in 2021. Time. Retrieved November 11, 2022, from https://time.com/6144877/industry-pay-increases-2021/

11 Cox, J. (2021, November 10). Inflation has taken away all the wage gains for workers and then some. CNBC. Retrieved November 11, 2022, from https://www.cnbc.com/2021/11/10/inflation-has-taken-away-all-the-wage-gains-for-workers-and-then-some.html

Anecdotally, employers who have already increased wages have noticed some interesting trends:

- Increased labor costs can be offset by the reduction in turnover and talent acquisition costs [12]
- Workers are more loyal, more engaged, and provide better customer service [13]
- Communities rally behind local businesses that do right by their employees
- Workers who make a living wage with a single full-time job are likely to quit working multiple jobs to make ends meet

I would argue that we've had a worker shortage for much longer than we've realized. We just didn't notice because one person was working two or three low-wage jobs at a time. Now that same worker can make ends meet with a single full-time position. This leaves a vacancy (or two) for each person who drops the burden of a second (or third) job.

4. Direct and Indirect Impacts of Covid-19

Nearly 1 million Americans have died from Covid-19 as of this writing, approximately one quarter of whom had not yet reached retirement age.[14] These deaths alone may account for 250,000 open positions in the workforce, not to mention the devastating toll on families and communities.

At the same time, we can't forget that Long Covid may lead us to what Scientific American describes as "a tsunami of disability" among U.S. workers.[15] As many as one in four Americans already lived with a disability before the pandemic. Long Covid could add another 8 million or more people to those ranks. People with disabilities are less able to work by definition, but also struggle to secure jobs for which they are highly qualified.[16] Even a conservative estimate here could account for the full worker shortage.

12 Hammond, C. (2021, May 26). This pgh ice cream parlor pays $15/hr, filled all its positions, and didn't raise prices. how it happened - pennsylvania capital. Star. Retrieved November 11, 2022, from https://www.penncapital-star.com/covid-19/this-pgh-ice-cream-parlor-pays-15-hr-filled-all-its-positions-and-didnt-raise-prices/#:~:text=To%20kill%20two%20birds%20with,this%20change%20on%20April%201.

13 Piehler, L. (2017, May 31). Paying employees a living wage is good for business. Community First. Retrieved November 11, 2022, from https://carleton.ca/communityfirst/2017/paying-employees-living-wage-good-business/

14 Schreiber, M. (2022, March 29). What one million Covid dead mean for the U.S.'s future. Scientific American. Retrieved November 11, 2022, from https://www.scientificamerican.com/article/what-one-million-covid-dead-mean-for-the-u-s-s-future/

15 Pomeroy, C. (2021, July 6). A tsunami of disability is coming as a result of 'long covid'. Scientific American. Retrieved November 11, 2022, from https://www.scientificamerican.com/article/a-tsunami-of-disability-is-coming-as-a-result-of-lsquo-long-covid-rsquo/

16 Waninger, A. (2022, April 19). Neurodivergent, disabled, and highly qualified for the job. Lead at Any Level®. Retrieved November 11, 2022, from https://leadatanylevel.com/neurodivergent-disabled-and-highly-qualified-for-the-job/

The Increasingly Unbearable Cost of Turnover

A recent Gartner survey reveals that 91 percent of HR leaders are concerned about employee turnover in the immediate future.[17] They're right to be worried. Depending on your industry, between one-quarter and one-third of your employees are looking for a new job right now.[18] CEOs and CFOs know that this level of turnover both limits growth and undercuts profits. In fact, turnover costs your company more than you may realize.

Empty Seats Don't Deliver

You don't have to be in the widget business to see how an empty seat affects productivity. Client project delays can damage relationships and reputations. Late delivery of an internal project has ripple effects on other departments, product quality, or market share. For public-facing roles, an open position may limit your capacity to sell, serve, or (in the case of hospitals) save lives. When the open seat belongs to a management or leadership role, teams suffer from a lack of direction and often feel disconnected from the company's mission.

With overall unemployment around 3.4 percent ("full employment" is considered to be 5.0 to 5.2 percent), it's clear that the competition for quality talent is fierce.[19, 20, 21] This is especially true in our clients' primary industries, where unemployment is even lower:

- Healthcare (2.7 percent)[22]
- Tech sector (2 percent)[23]
- Insurance industry (1.7 percent),[24] and financial services broadly (1.8 percent)[25]

17 Gartner Survey reveals 91% of HR leaders are concerned about employee turnover in the immediate future. Gartner. (2021, September 30). Retrieved November 11, 2022, from https://www.gartner.com/en/newsroom/press-releases/09-30-21-gartner-survey-reveals-ninety-one-percent-of-hr-leaders-are-concerned-about-employee-turnover-in-the-immediate-future
18 Gartner_Inc. (n.d.). Turnover risk is rising. or is it? size your risk. Gartner. Retrieved November 11, 2022, from https://www.gartner.com/en/articles/worried-about-employee-turnover-ask-these-6-questions-to-size-your-risk
19 United States unemployment rateoctober 2022 data - 1948-2021 historical. United States Unemployment Rate - October 2022 Data - 1948-2021 Historical. (n.d.). Retrieved November 11, 2022, from https://tradingeconomics.com/united-states/unemployment-rate#:~:text=The%20US%20unemployment%20rate%20edged%20up%20to%204.0%20percent%20in,persons%20declined%20by%203.7%20million.
20 U.S. Bureau of Labor Statistics. (n.d.). Full employment: An assumption within BLS Projections : Monthly Labor Review. U.S. Bureau of Labor Statistics. Retrieved November 11, 2022, from https://www.bls.gov/opub/mlr/2017/article/full-employment-an-assumption-within-bls-projections.htm#:~:text=BLS%20defines%20full%20employment%20as,GDP%20is%20at%20its%20potential.
21 Hartman, M. (2015, September 4). Does 5.1 percent = full employment? Marketplace. Retrieved November 11, 2022, from https://www.marketplace.org/2015/09/04/does-51-percent-full-employment/
22 U.S. Bureau of Labor Statistics. (n.d.). Industries at a glance: Health care and Social Assistance: NAICS 62. U.S. Bureau of Labor Statistics. Retrieved November 11, 2022, from https://www.bls.gov/iag/tgs/iag62.htm
23 Help Net Security. (2022, January 11). Technology-related employment still going strong, unemployment rate for it jobs dropping to 2%. Help Net Security. Retrieved November 11, 2022, from https://www.helpnetsecurity.com/2022/01/12/technology-employment/#:~:text=January%2012%2C%202022-,Technology%2Drelated%20employment%20still%20going%20strong%2C%20unemployment%20rate%20for,IT%20jobs%20dropping%20to%202%25
24 U.S. Bureau of Labor Statistics. (n.d.). Industries at a glance: Insurance carriers and related activities: NAICS 524. U.S. Bureau of Labor Statistics. Retrieved November 11, 2022, from https://www.bls.gov/iag/tgs/iag524.htm
25 U.S. Bureau of Labor Statistics. (n.d.). Industries at a glance: Finance and insurance: NAICS 52. U.S. Bureau of Labor Statistics. Retrieved November 11, 2022, from https://www.bls.gov/iag/tgs/iag52.htm

What does this mean for hiring managers? It's going to take longer and cost more to replace an employee who leaves.

Even after you hire a replacement, the new employee needs time to get up to speed. Learning the company culture, setting up their laptop, meeting new team members, navigating new processes, completing employment forms. These things take time. In some companies, it can take weeks just to get access to all the internal software needed to do the job, not to mention the time spent learning to use the software! That's just the start.

People who transfer from another department often need to learn new skills or procedures before they're fully productive. Someone who did the same job at another organization may need time to absorb the context of the new company or even a new industry. In other words, don't expect to fill your empty seat on Monday and be running at full capacity by Friday. It just doesn't work that way.

> *"Don't expect to fill your empty seat on Monday and be running at full capacity by Friday. It just doesn't work that way."*

Recruiting Costs Money and Takes Time

When a role needs to be filled, someone has to find candidates for the job. Recruiters don't work for free, nor should they! It takes a significant amount of time to write the posting, review resumes, screen candidates, schedule interviews, follow up, negotiate offers, verify references, and (in some cases) conduct background checks.[26, 27] Booths at job fairs, position listings on job boards, and ads on job sites all cost real dollars. A price that is likely to increase in such a hot market. Applicant tracking systems also cost money.

Hiring managers typically dread undertaking a selection process, and with good reason. They need time to develop selection criteria, assemble and onboard a selection committee, conduct interviews, compare candidates, and make final decisions. Multiply this effort by the rounds of interviews required and the number of candidates involved.

Hiring managers typically also manage the onboarding process (to the extent one exists), helping new hires obtain tax forms, login credentials, and needed training. Then there are dozens of introductions to be made and hundreds of unanticipated questions to be answered.

26 Waninger, A. C. (2018). Hire beyond bias: How to pick the best person for the job. Lead at Any Level, LLC.
27 Waninger, A. C. (2022, January 17). Calling bullshit on the "Pipeline Problem". Lead at Any Level®. Retrieved November 11, 2022, from https://leadatanylevel.com/pipeline-problem/

"Greener Grass Syndrome" is Contagious

Employees usually leave for a reason. They were bored or felt unappreciated in their role. The new company offered them double their current salary. Or their boss from three jobs ago called with an opportunity that spoke to their exact ambitions. Whatever the reason, something about the new opportunity appealed to them more than staying put did.

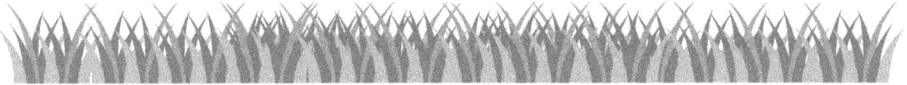

They won't tell you the truth about why they're leaving

Employees typically don't want to burn bridges with former employers. They may be evasive about "pursuing new opportunities" when the reality is much more concrete. You won't hear about the lack of development opportunities at the current company, or that they don't see a clear career path for themselves. They may not tell you that they're tired of the way a certain colleague derides them in meetings or takes credit for their work.

They probably *did* tell their colleagues exactly why

For example, if Pam learned she was making 25 percent less than her peer Jim, you can bet that every woman in your department has heard about it. If Rohit was offered a big promotion to move to a competitor, his colleagues are probably wondering what opportunities they're missing out on. The more egregious the reason, the more likely it's being talked about, and the less they're going to divulge that information through official channels.

I call this "Greener Grass Syndrome," and it is highly contagious. It infects the imagination of the departing employee long before they give their notice or pack up their desk. It also has the potential to spread to others on the team. Colleagues see their former peer thriving in a new role. They begin to think, "Maybe I should get my resume together. Am I really happy here? What's next for me?"

Contagion can reach catastrophic levels when a popular manager leaves. Why? Good managers tend to take great people with them. They may need a few weeks to get their footing in a new environment. They might have to wait out a non-compete clause. But eventually, they will call, saying, "Hey, it's great over here. Why don't you come?" And when they do, they probably know every single sore spot that employee has about their current role. They know exactly which buttons to push to win the employee over.

Let's be clear: the grass isn't always greener at a new company or in a new role. But when one of our peers moves on to a new pasture, it's hard for us not to want more opportunity for ourselves.

Burden Falls on the Team that Remains

Your team has noticed the work doesn't stop just because someone left.

What happens while you're backfilling that role? The work spreads out among the team. So now instead of eight widgets a day, each remaining team member needs to produce ten widgets a day to keep pace. The hours get longer; the work gets more intense.

Add to this burden that the people who remain are also sometimes responsible for finding and onboarding a replacement. On top of all the work that they already had, and the additional work that they're getting to try to keep pace because their peer has gone, you're also asking them to help with the selection process for a new colleague—something they're likely not trained in.

Multiply this frustration times the number of LinkedIn posts they're seeing from their former colleague, who's "excited to be starting a new journey." He's making more money, feels more appreciated, and doesn't have to deal with whatever drove him away in the first place.

A few more colleagues leave, and people start to wonder, "What does everybody else know that I don't?" Once this starts, it can take on a snowball effect that can be very difficult to contain.

Reputation Among Job Seekers

If you're a hiring manager, you've probably reviewed a resume or work history of someone you considered a "job hopper." You start to wonder, don't you, what is it about this person that makes them not stick with a job? How often did they change positions? Were they focused on upward mobility, are they never satisfied, do they not make good decisions, or are they difficult to work with? We tend to fill in the gaps with worst-case scenarios.

What we may not realize, though, is applicants have the same concerns about us and our companies. Especially when unemployment is this low, when there are more jobs than people available to fill the spots, and when wages are going up.

Employment culture is shifting. Worker expectations are changing. If job seekers see the same position posted for a long time—or posted several times over a few years—they may wonder, "What's wrong with that place?" Perhaps rightfully so.

Recommendations for Improving Engagement, Productivity, and Retention During the Current Labor Crisis

Your company is a diverse group of individuals with a common cause. In many ways, it acts like a family, with all the parts making a living, changing whole. Ultimately, regardless of any differences, everyone belongs. You want to keep them around. Retention is key. And at the heart of retention is the idea that the people you have feel like they are in the right place. That they are included.

Many executives tell me they want to "do something about diversity and inclusion" in their companies, but don't know where to begin. The steps are similar to those of any other major strategic initiative. But leaders tend to put off this work. Maybe their fear of doing the wrong thing keeps them from doing anything. Or maybe they think they can avoid the work altogether, just as they have always done.

If you are a leader who has shied away from creating an inclusive workplace, it's time to find your courage. Your workers can't wait another minute to feel valued in your organization.

Blueprint for Belonging™

A great place to start is to follow our Blueprint for Belonging™. This four-step process is actually a cyclical approach to increasing diversity and inclusion in your company in such a way that you actually continue to augment its efficacy and productivity.

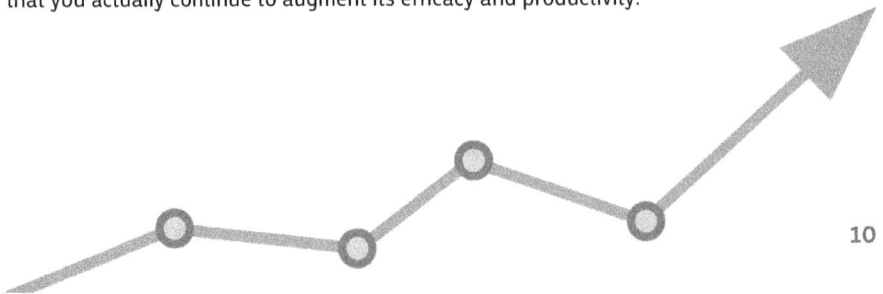

⟫LEAD AT ANY LEVEL®

Blueprint for Belonging™

Assess
- Quantitative (Data)
- Qualitative (Stories)

Target
- Business Case ("Why")
- Set Goals & Priorities

Plan
- Quick Wins
- Strategies & Milestones

Do
- Systems & Structures
- Training & Education

Step 1: Assess (Who feels included, who doesn't, and why?)

How do you know which direction to go, if you don't know where you are? Measuring diversity and inclusion may sound strange, but you need a starting point. Every organization's culture is inclusive for someone. But no culture is inclusive for everyone. You need to know who feels included, who doesn't, and why.

Diversity is easy to measure with demographic data. Comparing community, employee, and leadership demographics is a good place to start.

But how do you measure inclusion? That depends on whether you want quantitative data, qualitative data, or both.

For quantitative assessments, Lead at Any Level recommends the Spectra Diversity Inclusion Assessment (SDIA). It's the only statistically valid tool that measures both organizational and individual dimensions of inclusion in the same survey. [Lead at Any Level is an authorized delivery partner for the SDIA.] Quantitative assessments can help you establish broad baseline data, identify trouble spots, and measure progress over time.

Qualitative assessments, on the other hand, can help you understand the root cause of known problems. These projects typically involve both a review of company artifacts (such as policies and org charts) and a series of listening sessions (one-on-one interviews or focus groups).

Step 2: Target (Set your goals against informed baseline data)

Executives may react to assessment results in a variety of ways: surprised, angry, defensive, or reassured. Whatever the results, now is a good time for executives to reconnect to their organization's mission.

Align the "why" of your business with the "why" of this initiative. In doing so, you'll find the opportunities for improvement—and know how to communicate the changes to your employees.

When you know where you stand and what you stand for, it's easier to set goals and identify priorities. It's a baseline to answer questions like these:

- What do diversity and inclusion mean for your company?
- How will you know if you've accomplished your goal? Or if you're even on the right track?

Step 3: Plan

By this step, you know where you are and where you're headed. Now you can create your plan to get there. Identify some quick wins and execute them right away. Your employees will see that you're taking their feedback seriously.

You can't stop there! Choose long-term strategies carefully, always keeping your "why" in mind. Be sure to include interim milestones so you can celebrate victories along the way!

Step 4: Do

In this step, you have to move your feet consistently and determinedly toward your goal. You'll have a lot of options here for interventions. Be sure you're focused on both systemic changes and personnel development.

Expect to see improvements in morale, employee engagement, and employee retention. You can also expect resistance, frustration, and missteps. Growth is all part of the journey. If ever the process seems stale, or as if your organization is stuck, start again at Step 1 and assess where you are now.

Create Inclusive Leaders

How do you transform high-potential employees into effective, inclusive leaders? Do you change their titles, give them a bump in pay, assign some direct reports, and hope for the best? That's how a lot of organizations operate.

It probably won't surprise you to know that highly technical professionals—even the most talented ones—aren't usually born with all the skills they need to lead diverse teams effectively. Inclusive leadership requires us to release old ways of thinking, act with humility, and open ourselves to new perspectives.

These seven essential skills for inclusive leaders aren't often taught in college classrooms or corporate training spaces. They are vital to managing teams—and ourselves—through turbulence and into prosperity.

Understand Why Inclusive Leadership Matters

Have you ever wondered why so many companies focus on diversity and inclusion? You may be surprised to know that inclusive leaders can positively impact every aspect of company performance. From sales and marketing to supply chain, from operational efficiency to talent retention, inclusive organizations enjoy a sustainable competitive advantage. Inclusive leadership, therefore, drives bottom-line benefits and promotes a thriving organization.

GLOSSARY

- **Belonging** - *to feel happy and comfortable in a particular place or with a particular group of people*
- **Diversity** - *the fact that very different people or things exist within a group or place*
- **Engagement** - *emotional involvement or commitment*
- **Inclusion** - *the belief that all people should feel that they are included in society, even if they lack some advantages*
- **Productivity** - *the rate at which goods are produced, especially in relation to the time, money, and workers needed to produce them*
- **Retention** - *the ability to keep workers or customers from leaving a company, or students from leaving a school*
- **Turnover** - *the number of persons hired within a period to replace those leaving or dropped from a workforce or organization*

All definitions from Merriam-Webster.com. 2023. https://www.merriam-webster.com/dictionary/ and MacMillanDictionary.com. 2023. https://www.macmillandictionary.com/us/dictionary/ on 26 January, 2023.

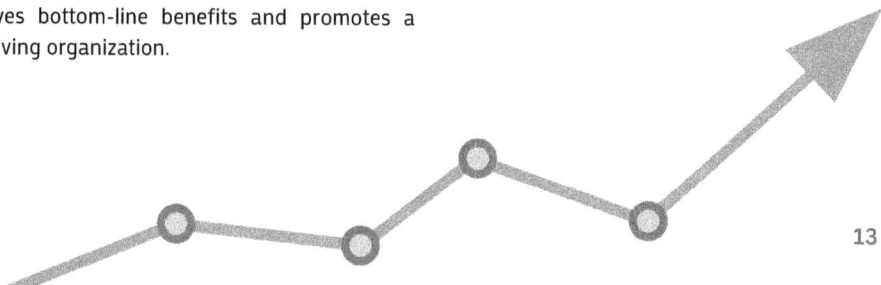

What would inclusive leadership allow you or your organization to do or become? Tie the work to your mission. Set measurable targets, and review progress regularly. That's how you keep your focus. (See Blueprint for Belonging above.)

Respond Productively to Change

Your industry is changing more rapidly than ever before, bringing a barrage of discussions about disruption, agility, and resilience. Professionals who adapt quickly can seize new opportunities and manage their careers.

Organizational change management focuses on "pushing" change outward. But leaders at every level need a foundation in consuming change responsibly. Learn techniques for identifying and overcoming fear, resistance, and uncertainty. Create action plans that put you in the driver's seat.

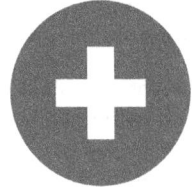

Build a Robust and Inclusive Professional Network

"Remember, we go far when we go together."

Is your professional network as diverse as the workforce and community around you? If not, you could be missing important opportunities for your career and your company.

We all face challenges in making meaningful connections. Inclusive leaders understand the impacts of these missed connections, then work to recognize and overcome them. Find ways to remove the artificial barriers that may be keeping you from your next mentor, star hire, or big customer. Then give them the opportunity to expand their networks as well.

Remember, we go far when we go together.

Focus on Strengths

No matter where you are in your career, you have the power to be a superstar. The key to your success lies in doing what you do best. For many of us, though, we take our gifts for granted and struggle to see what makes us uniquely talented. Take the time to recognize and celebrate how you (and others) can truly thrive! (As a Gallup-Certified Strengths Coach, I can't speak highly enough about the Gallup CliftonStrengths assessment.)

Once you've discovered your own strengths, you're ready to continue the journey and apply your talents in the real world.

Harness the collective power of your team. On strengths-based teams, everyone is valued for their strengths, while also recognizing that we need one another to realize individual and team excellence.

Give and Receive Feedback Effectively

Many people shy away from giving constructive feedback because they fear conflict. And while many are quick to praise for a job well done, few do so in a meaningful way.

Evidence shows that managers give the most (and the most useful) feedback to employees who are most similar to themselves. That won't do! Everyone deserves a chance to improve performance.

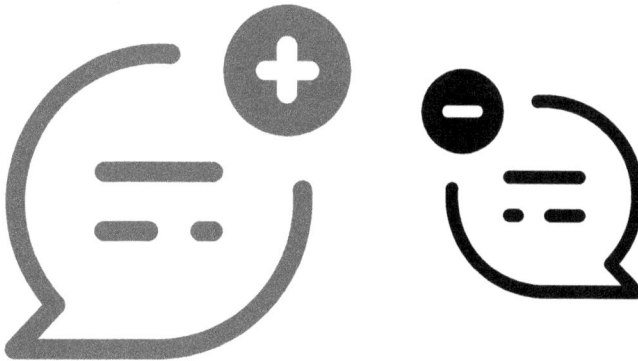

Use a consistent structure for giving feedback. Track the flow of feedback into, through, and beyond your team. Practice strategies for accepting both compliments and criticisms gracefully.

In time, you'll become confident coaching up, down, and across your organization. What's more, you and your leaders will be ready to seek out more meaningful feedback to propel your organization forward.

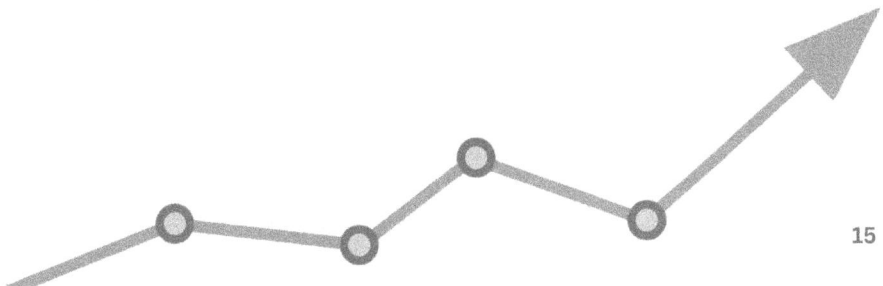

Hire the Right Person for the Job

Are you ready to expand your team or backfill an open position? Unconscious bias can influence our hiring processes in ways we don't readily recognize. This makes it hard for us to attract a diverse slate of candidates and to recognize qualified candidates who may not conform to our expectations. Leaders at every level of your organization, including individual contributors who conduct technical interviews, need to learn how to avoid common pitfalls at every stage of your selection process.

Create a Learning Culture

Ongoing professional development is an important component of a winning inclusive leadership strategy. But how do you influence your team or organization to adopt a "learning culture" that values professional excellence? Build and sustain an environment that supports your pursuit of lifelong learning.

Teams with learning cultures outperform other teams. Companies with learning cultures outperform their competitors. Keep developing these essential skills. The work of learning is never finished.

Inclusive Leaders Need Essential Skills Training!

We've combined our most popular keynotes and workshops to create a full year of leadership development programming, powered by the Lead at Any Level® Framework.

To learn more about Lead at Any Level's® *Essential Skills for Inclusive Leaders* developmental training, schedule time with us at www.workwithLAAL.com!

You Can't Wait...Here's Why

Everything Has Changed...

Let's indulge in a quick thought experiment. Jot down three quick answers to this prompt:

Name something that has changed about your company in the last five years.

Your answers might include:

External Factors:

- **What We Sell:** You've probably even updated the methods you use to research customer expectations.
- **Who We Serve:** Your customers themselves may have changed, or the market, or your target demographic may have shifted.
- **How We Market:** Brands are increasingly leveraging social media strategies to reach new audiences.
- **Who We Compete Against:** Online order systems and improved logistics have exposed even traditionally local businesses to global competition.
- **How We Deliver:** Digital subscriptions have replaced tangible products. Even many services can be delivered via Zoom or Teams, rather than in-person.
- **Our Vendors & Suppliers:** Global logistics have expanded our pool of suppliers, disruptions to global supply chains have forced some companies to diversify locally, and many customers demand we leverage diverse-owned and small businesses to comply with their strategic initiatives.

Internal Factors:

- **How We Communicate:** DMs, Slack and Discord channels, live video calls, and social media have changed the way we communicate with each other.
- **Where We Work:** Many of us now work remotely. Digital nomads can log in and produce results from nearly anywhere in the world.
- **The Jobs We Post:** Social Media Manager, Data Scientist, Python Developer, Virtual Assistant. These jobs didn't exist a few short years ago.
- **Who and How We Hire:** Demographic shifts, global talent markets, non-traditional training, and remote work have changed our talent pool. Recruiting looks different, especially as gig work increases and unemployment rates plummet.
- **How We Invest:** Investing has become more accessible to more people. Crowdfunding, cryptocurrency, and NFTs are recent examples of how investing has changed.
- **How We Get Work Done:** Internal processes, systems, and software have evolved. If you've heard the words "digital transformation" or "agile methodology," you can be sure that the way you work is changing.

...Except for Leadership (Probably)

Leaders at every level of your organization need to be on the cutting edge of change. But think about it:

- How have leaders in your organization adapted to all the changes we just discussed? Are they embracing the changes or waiting for a "return to normal"?
- Does your company define "leadership" differently than it did in the past?
- How have leaders in your organization historically been selected, evaluated, promoted, and trained? Which of these processes has changed to keep pace with the changing demands of your customers and talent pool?

...Which Brings Me to the Leadership Lie

This brings to the misguided axiom you may have heard from coaches and consultants in your industry:

If you do what you've always done,
you'll get what you've always gotten.
—Most Consultants

False! If it's not a leadership lie, then it's at least not the whole truth.

You can't get the same sales results doing what you used to do. The world has changed! Customers no longer call because they saw your ad in the yellow pages. You won't get the right job applicants by simply placing an announcement in the local newspaper. And you can't keep your employees happy and engaged with the same approach to leadership you used a decade ago.

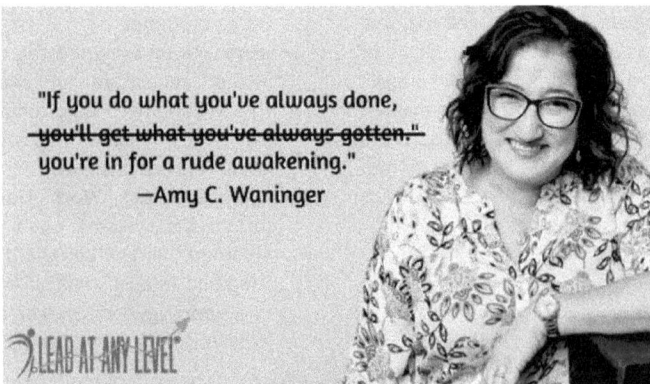

"If you do what you've always done,
~~you'll get what you've always gotten.~~
you're in for a rude awakening."
—Amy C. Waninger

LEAD AT ANY LEVEL

We need to ensure leaders value people in ways they haven't–and haven't been trained to–before. Our companies need to invest in leaders at every level to give them the skills they need today so they can adapt to the demands of tomorrow. Your employees and customers won't wait forever.

Final Thoughts

If corporate leaders assume "people are lazy," we take away any power we have to guard against the problem. After all, there's little we can do about other people's internal motivations. Instead, we need to recognize the complex and interconnected external forces at play. Only then can we change course internally to meet our economy's labor needs.

In the current talent environment, the less turnover you have, the better. The more you can do to prevent the turnover in the first place, the less it's going to cost you.

For example, new clients say to me, "We really want to do a better job of recruiting, especially diverse talent. We see that this is a problem in our organization." My first question to them is always "How are you ensuring that you keep the diverse talent you have on staff right now?" If more talent is going out than is coming in, you might as well be putting your recruiting dollars in a paper shredder.

Ninety percent of executives and HR leaders worry about turnover right now, and for good reason. If you're one of them, I urge you to do something about it now. The strategies outlined above are a great starting block to increase your company's diversity, inclusion, and retention. IIf you find that you need to take a deeper dive into addressing these issues, or you just don't know where to start, Lead at Any Level specializes in improving employee engagement and retention for companies that promote from within.

Schedule time with me at WorkWithLAAL.com. Let's work together so you can keep your employees—and keep them engaged.

About the Author

Amy C. Waninger (pronouns: she/her/hers) works with organizations that promote from within to help them keep their employees—and keep them engaged.

As the founder and CEO of Lead at Any Level®, Amy works with organizations to attract and retain diverse talent by developing inclusive leaders. She helps to build inclusive cultures and diverse leadership pipelines for a sustainable competitive advantage by offering assessment, advisory, and training services. Amy has been named a Top HR Influencer globally, and she has worked with clients and audiences on all seven continents-including Antartica!

Amy is the author of seven books, including Hire Beyond Bias: How to Pick the Best Person for the Job. Amy is a Professional Member of the National Speakers Association and a Prosci Certified Change Practitioner. Amy is a Certified Diversity Professional (CDP), a Certified Diversity Executive (CDE), and a Gallup-Certified Strengths Coach. Her other credentials include two degrees from Indiana University and a "World's Best Mom" coffee mug.

LEAD AT ANY LEVEL® Leaders can be anywhere, and should be *everywhere!*

(317) 589-5955
info@Leadatanylevel.com

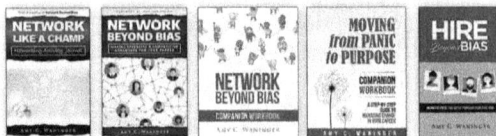

www.ingramcontent.com/pod-product-compliance
Lightning Source LLC
Chambersburg PA
CBHW060514200326
41520CB00017B/5041